ALMOST IMPOSSIBLE

NUMBER PUZZLES

The Puzzle Society™
puzzlesociety.com

Andrews McMeel
Publishing, LLC
Kansas City

09 10 11 12 13 WKT 10 9 8 7 6 5 4 3 2

ISBN-13: 978-0-7407-8092-9

ISBN-10: 0-7407-8092-1

Puzzles supplied under license from Arcturus Publishing.

www.andrewsmcmeel.com

www.puzzlesociety.com

ATTENTION: SCHOOLS AND BUSINESSES

Andrews McMeel books are available at quantity discounts
with bulk purchase for educational, business, or sales
promotional use. For information, please write to: Special
Sales Department, Andrews McMeel Publishing, LLC,
1130 Walnut Street, Kansas City, Missouri 64106.

Welcome to *Almost Impossible Number Puzzles*, a truly fiendish collection of mindbending puzzles designed to both test and entertain you.

The puzzles are tailored to inspire you and really get you thinking. Special knowledge is not required to solve them, neither do you need a degree in mathematics. We have included two of the latest puzzle crazes to arrive from Japan—Sudoku and Kakuro. Just in case you have not come across them before, following we have given you an easy-to-understand guide on how to solve them.

The answers to all the puzzles are provided at the back of the book, but try not to peek until you have had a really good attempt at solving a puzzle.

Almost Impossible Number Puzzles is a stimulating, challenging, but above all, fun way of sharpening your wits and training your mind to think logically. So, grab that pen and get ready for the time of your life!

How to Solve the Puzzles

Sudoku

Place a number from 1–9 in each empty cell so that each row, each column, and each 3 × 3 block contains all the numbers from 1–9.

Look at the central 3 × 3 block. You have to place a number 1, but it can't fall in the same row or column as any other 1. In this instance, there's only one available position for the 1. Using this method, you can quickly identify the positions of the other 1s.

Sudoku is simple to learn, requires no calculations, and provides a surprisingly wide variety of logical situations. No wonder it has become such a popular puzzle.

How to Solve the Puzzles

Kakuro

Fill the grid so that each block adds up to the total in the box above or to the left of it. You can only use the digits 1–9 and you must not use the same digit twice in a block. (The same digit may occur more than once in a row or column, but it must be in a separate block.)

Let's walk through a puzzle, touching on the main concepts.

As you begin, watch out for two things:
a) sums that are made up of unique digit answers (UDAs). See the table on page viii for guidance.
b) sums that are comprised of few cells.

Step One

On the right-hand side of the puzzle are two intersecting sums that are made up of two cells. The horizontal sum must add up to four. It can't be 2 and 2, because you can't repeat a digit in a sum, so it must be 1 and 3. But what's the order?

The vertical sum must add up to three, so is made up of 1 and 2. The only digit in both answers is a 1, so this must go in the intersecting cell, determining the positions of the 2 and 3.

Step Two

There is a 2 on the horizontal line that must add up to ten. That line is intersected by a sum that must add up to 3. We can't have another 2 in the horizontal line.

As the only combination for the three sum is 2 and 1, this means the intersecting cell must be a 1. The horizontal line beneath it also adds up to 3 and can be completed, too.

Step Three

On the horizontal line that totals ten, we have a 1 and a 2. The remaining two cells add up to 7. There are three possible combinations: 1 and 6; 2 and 5; and 3 and 4. We already have a 1 and 2 on the line, so the only available pair is 3 and 4.

The empty cell between the 1 and the 2 intersects with a sum that already contains a 3, so this cell must hold the 4. This means we can complete the horizontal ten sum and the intersecting ten sum.

Step Four

On the left-hand side are two more sums that are made up of two cells: the vertical sum is 14, the intersecting horizontal sum is 6. The only combinations for 14 are 9 and 5, and 8 and 6. The only possible digit that can intersect with the six sum is the 5.

Once you've placed the 5, the other digits that make up the sums can be fitted in.

Step Five

The horizontal line at the top of the puzzle has a five sum. The only two combinations are 1 and 4, and 2 and 3. As 1 and 3 appear already in the intersecting eleven sum, the only possible digits are 2 and 4. If it was a 4, the remaining digit in the eleven sum would be a 3, but there's a 3 in that sum already, so the horizontal sum must be 2 and 3, in that order.

To finish: 1 completes the vertical 4 sum and a 5 completes the vertical eleven sum.

Unique Digit Answers

For certain sums, only one combination of digits is
possible. Here's a useful table of Unique Digit Answers.
Look out for these in the Kakuro puzzles that follow.
They'll be a great help.

Sum Numbers

3	1•2
4	1•3
16	7•9
17	8•9
6	1•2•3
7	1•2•4
23	6•8•9
24	7•8•9
10	1•2•3•4
11	1•2•3•5
29	5•7•8•9
30	6•7•8•9
15	1•2•3•4•5
16	1•2•3•4•6
34	4•6•7•8•9
35	5•6•7•8•9

21	1•2•3•4•5•6
22	1•2•3•4•5•7
38	3•5•6•7•8•9
39	4•5•6•7•8•9
28	1•2•3•4•5•6•7
29	1•2•3•4•5•6•8
41	2•4•5•6•7•8•9
42	3•4•5•6•7•8•9
36	1•2•3•4•5•6•7•8
37	1•2•3•4•5•6•7•9
38	1•2•3•4•5•6•8•9
39	1•2•3•4•5•7•8•9
40	1•2•3•4•6•7•8•9
41	1•2•3•5•6•7•8•9
42	1•2•4•5•6•7•8•9
43	1•3•4•5•6•7•8•9
44	2•3•4•5•6•7•8•9
45	1•2•3•4•5•6•7•8•9

Questions

1 The diameter of pulley E is twice that of pulley D. If gear A rotates eight times clockwise, how many times will pulley E rotate and in what direction?

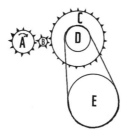

2 A What number starts the top series?
B What number ends the bottom series?

A — 8 1 6 3 2 6 4 1 2 8
B 1 9 3 8 7 6 1 5 2 3 0 —

3 What is the last line?

9 7 5 9 4 9
6 3 4 5 3 6
1 8 2 0 1 8

_____

4 In a game of bridge, GEORGE partnered MARY, while TED had to select a partner from ANN, EDNA, JOAN, or ANGELA. Whom did he choose?

5 Which of these contains the most triangles?

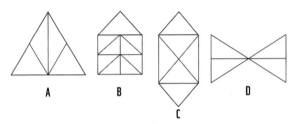

A   B   D

C

6 What comes next?

6 1 3 1 4 —

7 The combined age of Alan and Bertie is 43. The combined age of Alan and Charlie is 55. The combined age of Bertie and Charlie is 66.

How old are Alan, Bertie, and Charlie?

8 How can you make this addition correct?

$$
\begin{array}{r}
11 \\
66 \\
88 \\
\underline{96} \\
294
\end{array}
$$

9 The numbers in what two rows can be reversed so that the total of each row—across and down—equals 10?

A 5 4 1
B 6 1 3
C 3 5 2

10 What goes into the empty brackets?

1 2 [2 8 4 6] 3 4
4 5 [1 2 2 1 1 5 1 8] 6 7
7 8 [2 8 4 0 3 2 3 6] 9 10
11 12 [– – – – – – – –] 13 14

11 What number should replace the question mark?

4	5	1
2	?	5
4	2	4

12 Frank has half as many again as Sally, who has half again as many again as Mary. Altogether they have 209.

How many has each?

13 What comes next in the sequence?

> **346**
>
> **289**
>
> **134**
>
> **628**
>
> **?**

14 How many minutes before 12:00 noon is it if 72 minutes ago it was twice as many minutes past 9:00 A.M.?

15 Each letter points to a row of six numbers
Which is the odd one out?

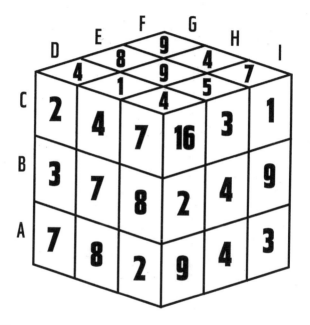

16 Starting at midnight, snow fell 1½" every 6 hours. If there was already 2¼" of snow at midnight, what was the thickness of the snow at 9:00 A.M.?

17 Sudoku

		7	3					9
	2				5			
1			7			3		
9			5					8
		6	8		4	1		
3					1			7
		5			3			1
			1				2	
6					7	4		

18 What is the sum of the numbers in the following list that are consecutive (for example 3, 4, 5)?

15	5	10	28
24	7	18	26
11	21	17	13
22	9	1	20

19 What number should replace the question mark?

7	8	9
4	6	8
1	?	7

20 Which arithmetic signs should go into the brackets to complete the equations?

A 5 [ ] 5 [ ] 5 = 2
B 4 [ ] 4 [ ] 4 = 4
C 3 [ ] 3 [ ] 3 = 6
D 2 [ ] 2 [ ] 2 = 8

21 What number should replace the question mark?

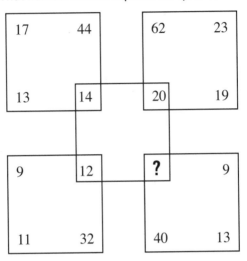

22 What belongs in the empty brackets?

6	3	[5	9	4	2]	7	1
5	9	[7	1	6	3]	4	2
9	4	[4	2	5	9]	2	8
		[–	–	–	–]		

23 What is two-sevenths of five-ninths of three-eighths of 168?

24 Every brick in this pyramid contains a number that is the sum of the two numbers below it, so that F=A+B, etc. Just work out the missing numbers!

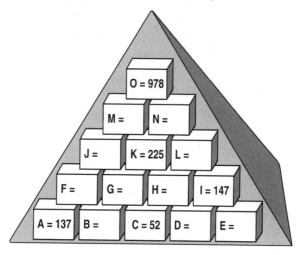

O = 978

M =   N =

J =   K = 225   L =

F =   G =   H =   I = 147

A = 137   B =   C = 52   D =   E =

25 What number should replace the question mark?

2	7
1	6

7	8
5	?

5	1
4	2

26 Kakuro

27 The seventh batter out in the innings scored 36 runs, which raised the average for all seven batters from 15 to 18. How many runs would the seventh batter need to score to raise the average to 20?

28 What is **X**?

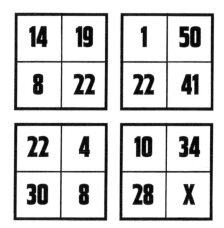

14	19
8	22

1	50
22	41

22	4
30	8

10	34
28	X

29 What belongs in the empty brackets?

```
2      [3  8]        3
4   [1  5  2  4]     5
6   [3  5  4  8]     7
8   [            ]   9
```

30 What number should replace the question mark?

7	6	5	23
9	2	8	7
6	14	2	22
4	8	7	?

31 The opposite faces of a die add up to seven. The dice below rotate in the directions indicated, one face at a time. After three moves, what will be the total of the front face?

32 Simplify by working each stage progressively:

$$16 - 20 \times 2 + 40 \div 8 + 19 = x$$

33 The average of two numbers is 41½. The average of three numbers is 72. What is the third number?

34 Sudoku

1		4					5	
			2		6	9		
			3					
	2							
7				4				8
							3	
			8					
		3	7		5			
	6					2		1

35 In the game of snooker, a player must pot a red ball each time before potting a "colored" ball (that is, a ball other than red). Each red ball scores 1 point; the "colors" score as follows:

Yellow–2
Green–3
Brown–4
Blue–5
Pink–6
Black–7

If a player potted two blacks, one yellow, one blue, and then two brown balls, followed by one red ball, what would the score be?

36 Multiple Choice:

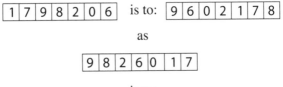

| 1 | 7 | 9 | 8 | 2 | 0 | 6 | is to: | 9 | 6 | 0 | 2 | 1 | 7 | 8 |

as

| 9 | 8 | 2 | 6 | 0 | 1 | 7 |

is to:

A | 1 | 8 | 7 | 0 | 9 | 6 | 2 | C | 2 | 7 | 1 | 0 | 9 | 8 | 6 |

B | 7 | 2 | 1 | 6 | 0 | 9 | 8 | D | 6 | 8 | 7 | 1 | 9 | 2 | 0 |

37 What number should replace the question mark?

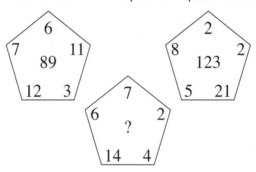

38 All of these except one have one thing in common. Which is the odd one out?

A   **764345896**

B   **125612456**

C   **367874341**

D   **456578325**

E   **178652457**

F   **279651238**

39 Kakuro

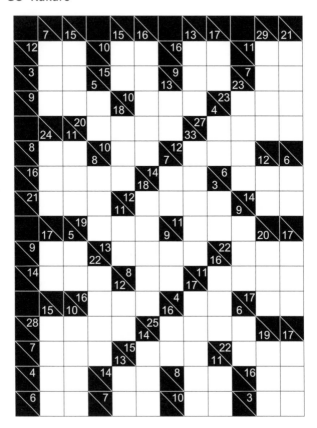

40 You have accidentally left the plug out of the drain and are attempting to fill the bath with both taps wide open. The hot tap takes 5 minutes to fill the bath and the cold tap 4 minutes. The water completely drains in 20 minutes.

In how many minutes will the bath be filled?

41 How many circles appear below?

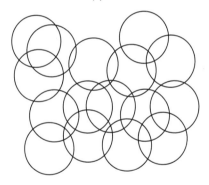

42 Simplify:

$$\frac{9}{72} \div \frac{36}{144} \div \frac{12}{36}$$

43

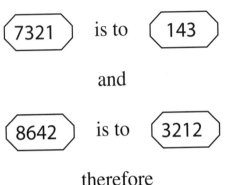

7321   is to   143

and

8642   is to   3212

therefore

5126   is to   ?

44 What number should replace the question mark?

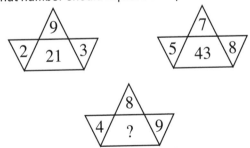

45 Sudoku

8					7	1		
	3	1					4	
			1		6		2	
							5	
	6		2	7	9		1	
	9							
	2		3		4			
	1					8	6	
		5	6					4

46 Which number is the odd one out?

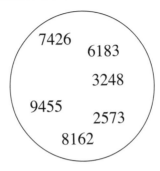

7426
6183
3248
9455
2573
8162

47 What is the total of the numbers on the reverse side of these dice?

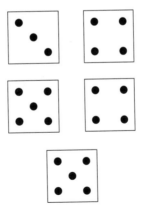

48 You have 13 diamond cards:

Ace 2 3 4 5 6 7 8 9 10 Jack Queen King

What are the chances of drawing King, Queen, Jack, and 10 in that order?

49 Each symbol ♡ ♧ ◇ ♤ has a value. Which symbol should replace the question mark to make the totals correct?

♡	♤	♧	♧	28
♡	◇	◇	◇	26
♡	♤	♤	♧	21
♡	♧	♧	?	32
44	15	22	26	

50 A feature of many safe-driving competitions consists of a row of poles set at varying distances from each other, ranging from narrow to wide. Maximum points are scored if the driver chooses the narrowest gap through which he can drive without touching a pole. Thus, the driver must relate the width of his car to the width between the poles. In a competition between drivers A and B, which gap should each driver choose?

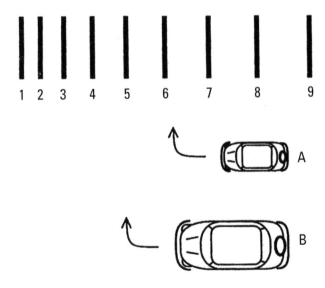

51 Which number should replace the question mark?

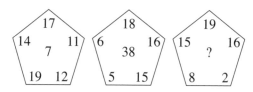

52 What number is three places away from itself plus 3, two places away from itself multiplied by 4, three places away from itself less 2, two places away from itself plus 8, and three places away from itself less 1?

52	24	30	9	16
5	3	21	12	2
18	45	4	36	7
13	11	8	16	50
40	6	10	15	1

53 Can you place the hexagons into the grid, so that where any hexagon touches another along a straight line, the contents of both triangles are the same? No rotation of any hexagon is allowed!

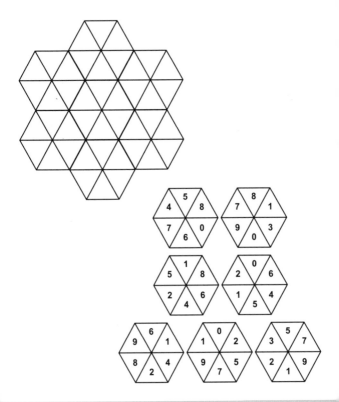

54 The answer is 12. Why?

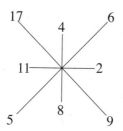

55 Which numbers will replace the question marks?

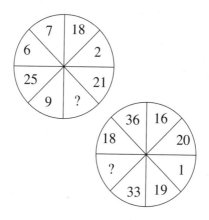

56 What two numbers continue the sequence?

4 1 9 2 15 4 22 7 ? ?

57 Kakuro

58 What numbers are represented by A, B, and C?

A	B	A	B	A	23
B	C	A	A	A	20
B	A	B	C	A	24
B	A	C	C	A	21
B	B	A	A	B	27
31	**24**	**20**	**21**	**19**	

59 You have a range of weights available, from 1 to 10 units. They are all single weights.

Which one should you use to balance the scale, and where should you place it?

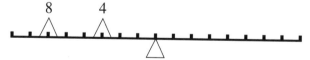

60 If a group of 6 people have an average age of 21, and each person is half the age of the next person, what are the ages of the 6 people?

61 What number should replace the question mark?

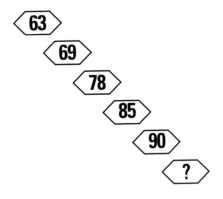

62 What comes next in the series?

1072 1055 1021 953 817 545 –

63 What number is missing?

469257   296412   ?   9645   699

64 What number should replace the question mark?

17	14	5	16
11			1
?			12
21	9	17	19

65 Puss had been called in to Monravia to get rid of the rats. Puss had been told that he could bring as many of his friends as he wished to help him. After a year every cat had killed an equal number of rats; the total was 1,111,111 rats.

How many cats were there?

66 What replaces the question mark?

| 4096 | 4913 | 5832 | ? |

67 Find the values for A, B, C, and D.

C	C	A	D	=22
C	D	D	A	=20
A	A	D	D	=32
C	B	B	A	=30

=24 =25 =23 =32

68 At the casino I had to pay a $1 entrance fee. I also gave the cloakroom girl a $1 tip each evening as I left. Each day for four days I lost half of the money I had left. I went home with $1. How much did I have to start with?

69 Which domino replaces the question mark to complete the puzzle?

70 Draw in the missing hands on the final clock.

71 Which shape has the greatest total degrees in its angles, and by how much?

72 Can you place the hexagons into the grid, so that where any hexagon touches another along a straight line, the contents of both triangles are the same? No rotation of any hexagon is allowed!

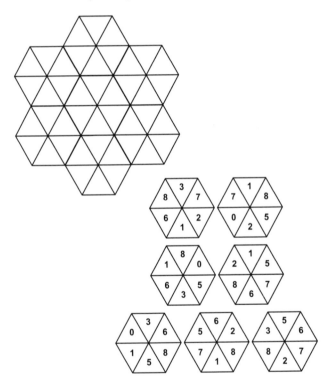

73 Sudoku

		5						
	1			8				4
9			3		6		8	
		4	9	7			1	3
1	3			2	4	9		
	6		1		2			9
3				9			7	
					5			

74 In the diagram below, which number should replace the question mark?

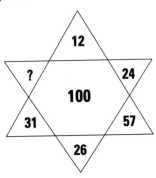

75 What number should replace the question mark?

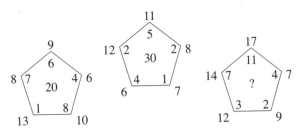

76 What is four-ninths of one-third of three-fifths of 1215?

77 Sudoku

	4						7	
	3		4				5	8
		5			6			9
5				2	7			
	8						1	
			9	1				3
1			8			2		
7	6				3		9	
	9						6	

78 The answer is 156. Why?

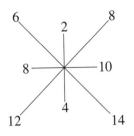

79 If you simplify

$$(89^2) - (88^2)$$

what is the correct answer?

A 176   **D** 179
B 177   **E** 180
C 178

80 Add the two highest numbers and take away the sum of the three lowest numbers.

16	13	9
11	23	19
5	14	12
15	18	17

81 What number should go under the letter E?

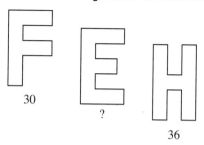

30

?

36

82 What number should replace the question mark?

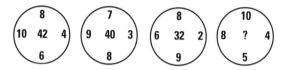

83 A car travels 40 miles in the same time as another car traveling 20 mph faster covers 60 miles.

How long does the journey take?

84 Which is the odd man out and why?

3	11	17
7	15	29

85 Draw in the missing hands on the final clock.

86 How many times must the large cog revolve before all of the cogs are in their original position?

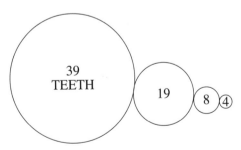

87 Kakuro

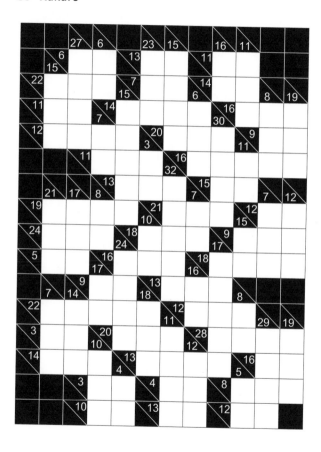

88 In the square below, change the positions of six numbers, one per row, column, and long diagonal line of six smaller squares, so that the numbers in each row, column, and long diagonal line total exactly 96.

14	9	10	23	14	14
25	26	18	21	30	4
22	9	12	28	21	10
21	9	30	4	17	24
9	8	6	11	32	6
14	23	26	2	10	14

89 The odometer in the car showed 15951 miles, a palindromic number.

Two hours later the odometer was once again palindromic.

How far had the car traveled?

90 What numbers should replace the question marks?

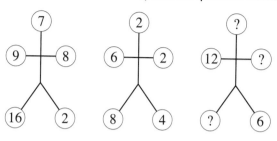

91 Alan has thought of a number between 13 and 1300. Bob is trying to guess it.

1 Bob asks whether the number is below 500. Alan says "yes."

2 Bob asks if the number is a perfect square. Alan says "yes."

3 Bob asks if the number is a perfect cube. Alan says "yes."
Alan says "only two of my answers are correct."
Alan says (truthfully) "the number starts with 5, 7, or 9."
Bob now knows the number.

What is it?

92 What number should replace the question mark?

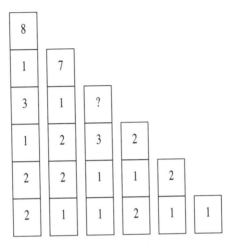

93 What should the time be on Clock D?

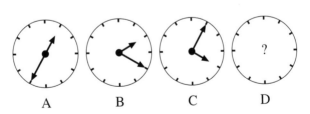

A   B   C   D

94 Which is the odd one out?

A 9 8 6 3 1 4 7
B 6 1 5 3 2 0 3
C 4 7 9 0 1 8 2
D 1 6 7 2 1 0 4
E 3 2 4 4 2 8 6
F 4 6 7 3 1 1 2
G 7 8 8 1 1 9 4

95 A heavy smoker, worried about the high cost of tobacco, decided to economize by saving his cigarette ends and making new cigarettes from them.

He found that each cigarette end accounted for one-sixth of the whole cigarette.

He smoked 36 cigarettes a day.

By using this method, how many extra cigarettes was he able to obtain in a week?

96 What number should replace the question mark in order to continue the sequence?

100   96   88   72   40   ?

97 Sudoku

	9				5			7
							6	
		2	8		3			
1								4
	7			9			5	
6								3
			4		2	9		
	5							
3			1				8	

98 Which is the missing tile?

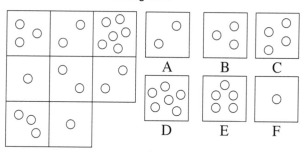

99 Which number should replace the question mark?

100 What number should replace the question mark?

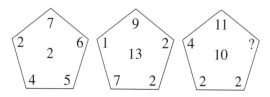

101 Which number comes next to a definite rule?

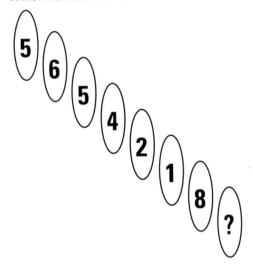

102 Two square floors had to be tiled, covered in 12" square tiles. The number of tiles used was 850 total.

Each side of one floor was 10' more than the other floor.

What were the dimensions of the two floors?

103 What is **X**?

3   6   10   15   **X**   28

104 Give values for **X** and **Y**.

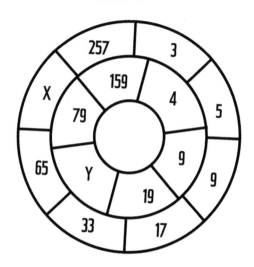

105 Multiply the second highest number by the second lowest number and then divide the result by the third lowest number.

10	35	2	32	37	33	9
13	36	12	14	34	3	11

106 How many 4-card permutations (arrangements) can you make in a pack of 52 standard playing cards?

107 Cyril lives on a road where the houses are numbered 8 to 100. John decided to visit, but didn't know which number Cyril lived at, so he asked him the following questions:

John asks "Is it greater than 50?"
Cyril answers "yes."

John asks "Is it a square number?"
Cyril answers "yes."

John asks "Is it an odd number?"
Cyril answers "yes."

John asks "Is the first digit an 8?"
Cyril lies.

What is the number of the house belonging to Cyril?

108 Which date does not conform with the others?

A	1417	D	1722
B	1533	E	1812
C	1605	F	1902

109 Kakuro

110 What comes next?

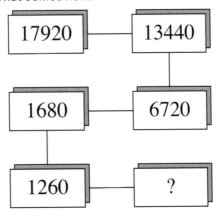

111 What number should replace the question mark?

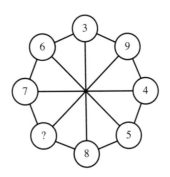

112 What are **X** and **Y**?

1 3 3 6 5 9 7 12 X Y

113 Draw in the missing hands on the final clock.

114 Tanya can swim faster than Jack but slower than Sally. Harry swims faster than Jack, sometimes swims faster than Tanya, but never swims faster than Sally. Who is the slowest swimmer?

115 If the temperature rises 15% from X°F to 103½°F, what was the previous temperature?

116 Which of the four lettered alternatives (A, B, C, or D) fits most logically into the empty square?

24	17	12
18	20	10
33	31	27

15	13	18
9	20	10
28	30	21

9	19	27
19	20	4
17	9	18

25	13	17
17	20	40
42	24	16

A

26	25	14
20	20	18
20	8	31

B

16	22	27
35	20	14
18	7	25

C

44	15	10
28	20	23
30	6	24

D

117 Sudoku

			2				1	
	3							4
	9			7				
2								7
		4		3		5		
1								6
				5			9	
8							2	
	6				4			

118 What number should replace the question mark?

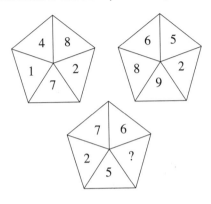

119 What number should replace the question mark?

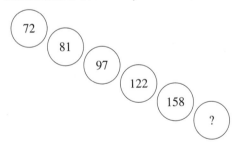

120 Divide 600 by $\frac{1}{4}$ and add 15. What is the answer?

121 How many revolutions must the largest cog make in order to bring the cogs back to their original positions?

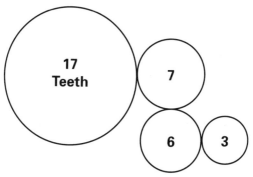

122 What number should go into the blank space?

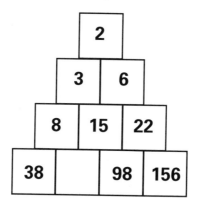

123 Which one is wrong?

A $\quad 9/4 + 1.75 = 4$

B $\quad 9/5 + 2.2 = 4$

C $\quad 6/5 + 2.8 = 4$

D $\quad 6/4 + 1.5 = 4$

E $\quad 9/6 + 2.5 = 4$

124 What number should replace the question mark?

```
      26                    14
31 ( 38 ) 9        12 ( 14 ) 5
      10                     7

      21                    17
11 ( 21 ) 2         9 ( ? ) 1
       9                    10
```

125 What numbers belong to A and B?

```
36  (35)  60
65  (58)  104
A   (79)  B
```

126 What number should replace the question mark?

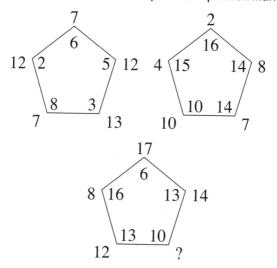

127 What is the difference between the lowest number and the average of all the numbers below?

3 9 12 15 18 25 30

128 What numbers should replace the question marks?

5 10 11 22 24 48 51 ? ?

129 What number should replace the question mark?

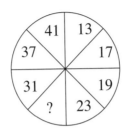

130 What number should replace the question mark?

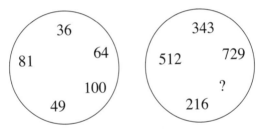

131 Square the lowest even number and subtract the result from the third highest odd number:

9	67	4	11	58	66
2	65	1	8	10	41
6	71	5	12	25	3
7	41	32	70	69	68

132 Draw in the missing hands on the final clock.

133 What number should replace the question mark?

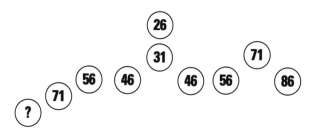

134 Which number should replace the question mark?

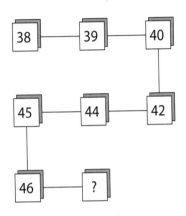

135 What is **X**?

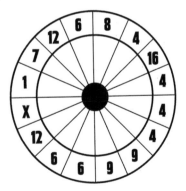

136 Kakuro

137 Draw in the missing hands on the final clock.

138 What is **X**?

139 What number should replace the question mark?

140 The cost of hiring a private rail car is shared equally by all the passengers who all paid an exact number of dollars, which was less than $100. The car has seats for 50 passengers and the total bill amounts to $1887.

How many seats were not occupied?

141 At the dog show the dogs' numbers were:

Corgi 11   Terrier 15   Whippet 17   Alsatian ?

What was the Alsatian's number?

142 What number should replace the question mark?

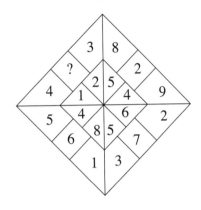

143 Add the sum of the odd numbers in square A to that of the even numbers in square B and subtract the sum of the prime numbers in square C.

4	7	9
18	26	2
3	5	15

A

8	10	7
3	1	2
14	13	6

B

6	15	17
3	9	4
21	11	19

C

144 The die below is rolled one face to square 2 and so on, one face at a time, to squares 3, 4, 5, and 6. Which number will appear on the top face in square 6?

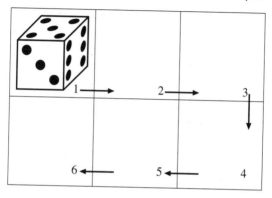

145 What number should replace the question mark?

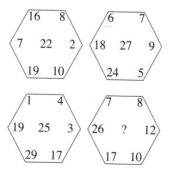

146 Sudoku

		1	8		2			
4					7		8	
		3				7		6
						4		
		7	9	5	1	3		
		9						
3		2				8		
	6		5					3
			7		3	1		

147 What weight should be placed at the question mark in order to balance the scales?

148 What number should replace the question mark?

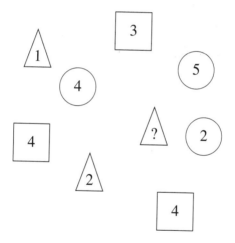

149 What comes next?

2   4   6   9   12   15   19   ?

150 Can you fill each square in the bottom line with the correct digit?

Every square in the solution contains only one digit from each of the lettered lines above, although two or more squares in the solution may contain the same digit.

At the end of every row is a score, which shows:

a) the number of digits placed in the correct finishing position on the bottom line, as indicated by a check; and

b) the number of digits which appear on the bottom line, but in a different position, as indicated by an x.

					SCORE
A	1	2	3	4	✗ ✗
B	2	5	4	6	✗ ✗
C	5	4	7	1	✓
D	3	8	2	4	✓ ✗
E	4	8	6	2	✓ ✓
					✓✓✓✓

151 Kakuro

152 Can you place the hexagons into the grid, so that where any hexagon touches another along a straight line, the contents of both triangles are the same? No rotation of any hexagon is allowed!

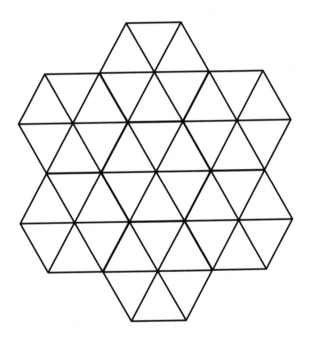

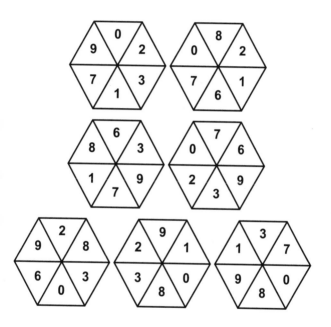

153 Which numbers should replace the question marks?

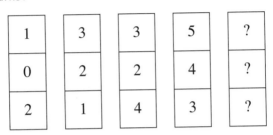

154 Simplify:

$$\frac{46}{27} \div \frac{92}{9} =$$

155 Five friends live on the same road in houses A, B, C, D, and E. The house numbers run from 4 to 36.

The numbers of houses B, C, D when multiplied together equals 1260. The numbers of houses B, C, D when added together equal twice E's number.

A's number is half as much again as E's.

What are the 5 house numbers?

156 Given that the letters are valued 1 through 26 according to their places in the alphabet, can you crack the mystery code to reveal the missing letter?

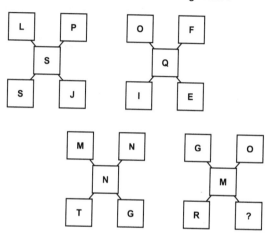

157 What number should replace the question mark?

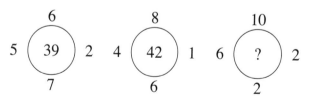

158 Can you fill each square in the bottom line with the correct digit?

Every square in the solution contains only one digit from each of the lettered lines above, although two or more squares in the solution may contain the same digit.

At the end of every row is a score, which shows:

a) the number of digits placed in the correct finishing position on the bottom line, as indicated by a check; and

b) the number of digits which appear on the bottom line, but in a different position, as indicated by an x.

SCORE

A	1	2	3	4	✗ ✗
B	5	3	6	1	✓ ✗
C	4	7	5	3	✓ ✗
D	8	3	6	7	✓ ✗
E	2	8	7	4	✓ ✗
					✓✓✓✓

159 What number should replace the question mark?

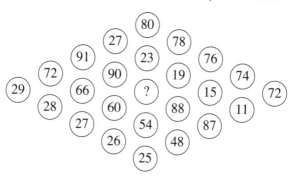

160 A hundred eggs are in a crate. If you draw out 2, and there are 6 bad eggs in the crate, what are your chances of drawing out 2 bad eggs?

161 At a school outing:

81% of the boys had lost a shoe;

82% of the boys had lost a sock;

77% of the boys had lost a handkerchief;

68% of the boys had lost a hat.

What percentage at least must have lost all 4 items?

162 Sudoku

				1		7	9	
3					8			
						5		
			1		4			8
		6		9		1		
5			3		6			
		9						
			2					4
	7	1		6				

163 What number should replace the question mark?

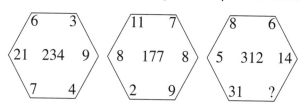

164 What are **X** and **Y**?

3 7 4 6 21 12 12 84 36 24 420 X Y

165 Give values for **X** and **Y**:

$$2X - Y = 5$$
$$X + Y = 16$$
$$Y - X = 2$$

166 How much does a box weigh if its weight is:

   A 999 lbs plus half its own weight

   B 999 lbs minus half its own weight

   C 999 lbs times half its own weight

   D 999 lbs divided by half its own weight

167 What number should be placed at the question mark to balance the scale?

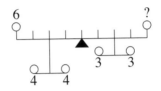

168 247 is to 494, as 538 is to which one of the three options shown below?

264   **219**   **269**

169 Fill the three empty squares with the symbols +, −, and x in some order, to make a sum which totals the number at the end. Each symbol must be used once and calculations are made in the direction of travel (left to right).

21 ☐ 6 ☐ 11 ☐ 5 = 80

170 What are **X** and **Y**?

72 7 36 14 18 28 9 56 X Y

171 Three basketball players were discussing their scores:

GEORGE:
"I scored 9; I scored 2 less than Henry; I scored 1 more than Malcolm."

HENRY:
"I did not score the lowest; the difference between my score and Malcolm's was 3; Malcolm scored 12."

MALCOLM:
"I scored less than George; George scored 10; Henry scored 3 more than George."

Each man had made one incorrect statement out of three.

What were the scores?

172 Multiply by 7 the number of odd numbers that are immediately followed by an even number in the list below.

4 9 6 2 3 4 7 8 2 1 9 6 4 3 2

What is the answer?

173 Every station on the railway system sells tickets to every other station. Some new stations were added. Forty-six sets of additional sets of tickets were required.

How many new stations have been added?

How many stations were there originally?

174 What should replace the question marks?

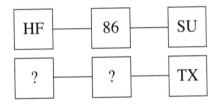

175 What should replace the question mark?

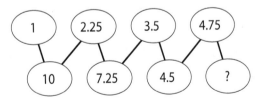

176 Kakuro

177 During a round of golf, my friend had scored a hole in one. There were 5 witnesses.

Here is a list of their statements about which hole produced the amazing feat. It was an 18-hole course.

A Not an even number.

B It had double digits.

C The number was made up of only straight lines.

D Not a prime number.

E Not a square number.

But only one statement was a true one.

Which hole was it?

178 What number should replace the question mark?

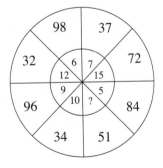

179 Find the starting point in the grid below and visit each square once only to reach the treasure marked T.

Clue: 1N 2W = 1 North, 2 West

2S 2E	1S 1W	1W 1S
2E 1N	T	1S 1W
1N 2E	2N 1W	2N 1W

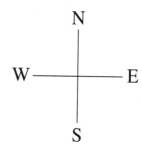

180 Among these dominoes how many double-sixes are there?

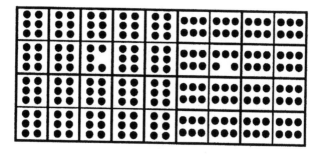

181 How many squares are there in this figure?

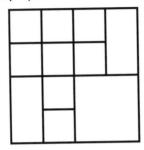

182 Which is the odd one out?

A	1	6	3	4	9	2
B	6	14	3	8	1	2
C	19	7	5	23	3	4
D	1	9	4	7	3	2

183 What is X?

X 11 1098 76 5 43 21

184 Simplify:

$$\frac{3}{4} \div \frac{27}{32} = ?$$

185 What is the ratio between A and C?

A   2 to 1
B   4 to 1
C   1 to 1
D   5 to 1

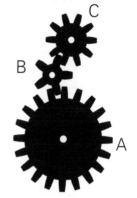

186 What number should replace the question mark?

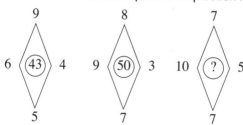

187 In 10 years' time the total ages for two brothers and two sisters will be 100.

What will the total be in 7 years' time?

188 Sudoku

				9				
			3		7			6
4		1					8	
	6							
		9		2		3		
							4	
	7					1		2
5			4		8			
				6				

189 What number should replace the question mark?

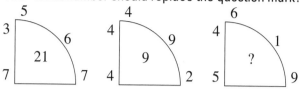

190 What number should replace the question mark?

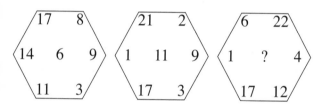

191 Which number in the top row belongs to the bottom row, and which number in the bottom row belongs to the top row?

9	25	49	81	96
8	12	121	18	14

192 A card player holds 13 cards of four suits, of which seven are black and six are red.

There are twice as many hearts as clubs and twice as many diamonds as hearts.

How many spades does he hold?

193 What is **X**?

131   517   192   X

194 Add the numbers that are squares of whole numbers to the prime numbers. What is the answer?

12	16	7	180	31
225	81	23	56	64
35	15	72	48	14

195 Find the weight to balance the scales.

196 What are **X** and **Y**?

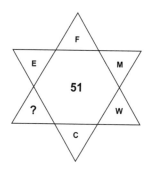

3	2
6	36

1	2
X	Y

1	4
4	16

197 In the diagram below, what letter should replace the question mark?

F

E

M

51

?

W

C

198 What are **X**, **Y**, and **Z**?

76 69 52 65 60 45 54 51 38
43 42 31 32 33 24 X   Y   Z

199 From a certain station a northbound train ran every ten minutes throughout the day; a southbound train also ran every ten minutes throughout the day.

A man went to the station every day at random times and caught the first train that arrived. On average he caught the northbound train nine times out of ten.

Why was this?

200 Draw in the missing hands on the final clock.

201 Kakuro

202 What time will this clock show in 3½ hours'
time, assuming it loses four seconds in every hour?
(State the exact time.)

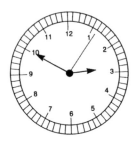

203 Multiply the square root of the highest number
by the square of the lowest number.

144	6	169	7	152
51	66	9	158	8
3	168	4	167	10

204 Out of 10 motors, 3 are defective. Two are
chosen at random. What are the chances that both
are defective?

205 What is **X**?

3	4	13
8	8	56
1	5	24
9	7	40
2	2	2
6	4	10
7	5	18
4	9	77
5	3	X

206 A turns clockwise, two positions at a time. B turns counterclockwise, three positions at a time. After six moves, what will be the total of the two front faces? (The concealed numbers progress in the same way as the visible numbers: 7, 9, and 11 on A; and 8, 10, and 12 on B.)

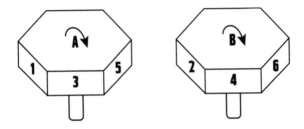

207 Which number from 1 to 9 is **X**?

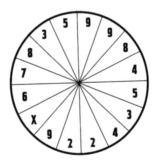

208 Fill the three empty circles with the symbols +, −, and x in some order, to make a sum that totals the number in the center. Each symbol must be used once and calculations are made in the clockwise direction.

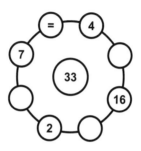

209 Insert the same number twice (not the number 1) to make this calculation correct.

$$6 \div 6 = 6$$

210 What is **X**?

1	2	3	2	10	12
2	5	12	10	16	13
1	2	1	X	10	24

211 Sudoku

		1	7		3			9
6				9		2		
							5	
7		6		3	8		9	
	8		9	2		7		6
	5							
		7		4				8
9			6		1	4		

212 Mr. Smith has a number of children.
Mr. Brown has a smaller number of children.
Mr. Green has an even smaller number of children.
Mr. Black has the smallest number.

The total is less than 18.
The product of the children is the door number of the Smiths' house (120).

I asked Mr. Smith: "Is there more than one child in the Black family?"
When he replied, as I knew the house number, I also knew the number of children in each family.

How many children were there in each family?

213 How many minutes is it before 12:00 noon if 132 minutes later it will be 3 times as many minutes before 3:00 P.M.?

214 Bill and Ben have a combined age of 91 years. Bill is now twice as old as Ben was when Bill was as old as Ben is now.

How old are Bill and Ben?

215 In the grid below, what number should replace the question mark?

23	25	9	4	22	23	30
16	18	3	8	6	22	12
8	7	8	4	18	13	6
33	10	13	11	4	15	5
12	2	13	29	12	1	4
1	15	26	31	19	16	14
5	21	26	11	?	8	27

216 What number should replace the question mark?

	3			7			?	
2		1	1		1	1		6
7		8	3		9	9		7

217 Fill in the two missing numbers.

5   (36)

4   (?) (?)

3   (57) (78) (93)

2   (15) (42) (36) (57)

1   (34) (19) (61) (25) (82)

218 What number should replace the question mark?

17   35   23   29   29   23   ?

219 How many triangles are in this figure?

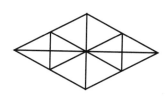

220 In how many circles does a dot appear?

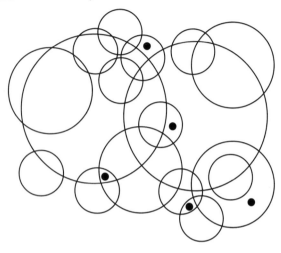

221 What number should replace the question mark?

222 Kakuro

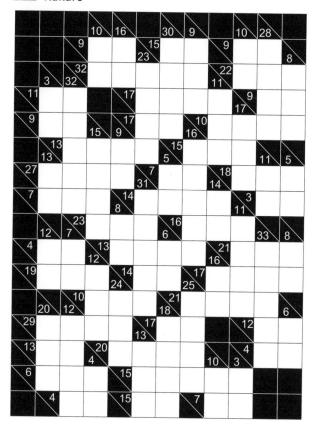

223 What is the value of the second line?

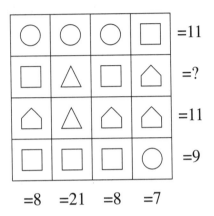

224 How many lines appear below?

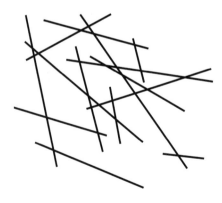

225 What number should replace the question mark?

$$7 \quad 17^1/_2 \quad ? \quad 109^3/_8$$

226 What number should replace the question mark?

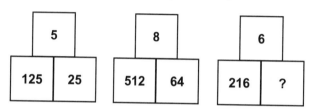

227 What is the only weight from 1 kilogram to 14 kilograms that cannot be weighed with the weights available?

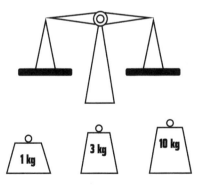

228 Can you place the hexagons into the grid, so that where any hexagon touches another along a straight line, the contents of both triangles are the same? No rotation of any hexagon is allowed!

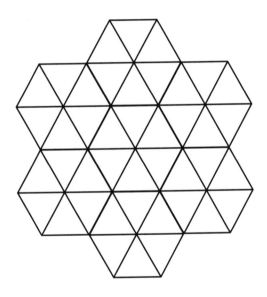

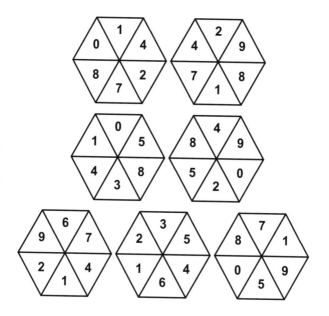

229 What number replaces the question mark?

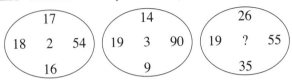

230 By which fraction does $^{19}/_{36}$ exceed a $^{1}/_{2}$?

231 What number should replace the question mark?

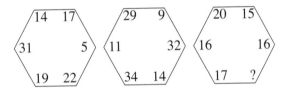

232 Two stations (A and B) have 4 stations between them. How many tickets must be issued so that a passenger can move from any station to another?

233 Sudoku

	7			1				
3	6		8					
	8	9			5			
			3	7		2		9
		5				4		
2		1		6	4			
			9			6	2	
					2		8	4
				8			7	

234 What number will replace the question mark?

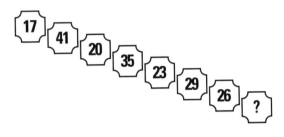

235 Simplify and find the value for **X**.

$$(3 \times 7) \times 14 - (8 - 5) - (12 \div 4) = X$$

236 What number should replace the question mark?

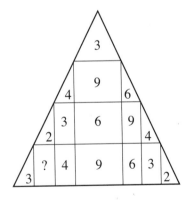

237 Kakuro

238 What is **X**?

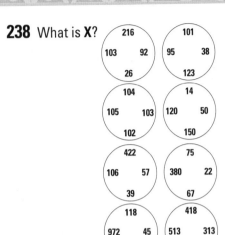

239 What number should replace the question mark?

7 9 $5\frac{3}{4}$ $10\frac{1}{4}$ $4\frac{1}{2}$ $11\frac{1}{2}$ **?**

240 At the state fair eating contest the winner ate an average of 15 hot dogs at the first 20 sittings. After a further 20 sittings the average increased to 20 hot dogs.

What was the average for the last 20 sittings?

241 Sudoku

						1	4	
9	1							2
		7	9		2			
			5	3			2	
1		5				6		4
	6			2	1			
			7		8	4		
8							5	6
	5	4						

242 Kakuro

243 What number should replace the question mark?

244 How many circles appear below?

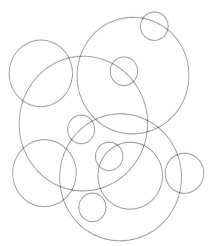

245 A train traveling at a speed of 80 mph enters a tunnel that is 0.5 miles long. The length of the train is 0.25 miles. How long does it take for all of the train to pass through the tunnel, from the moment the front enters, to the moment the rear emerges?

246 How many squares are there on an 8 × 8 chess board?

247 What number should replace the question mark?

$$
\begin{array}{ccc}
36 & (36) & 42 \\
54 & (25) & 49 \\
72 & (?) & 61
\end{array}
$$

248 In a horse race, the first 5 places were filled by horses 4, 1, 3, 2, and 5 in that order.

The jockey of horse 4 wore a green shirt, the jockey of horse 1 wore red, jockey 3 wore yellow, and jockey 2 wore orange.

Did jockey 5 wear purple, white, blue, or black?

249 What number should replace the question marks?

26, 61,
38, 82,
64, 45,
78, ??

250 Which playing card should replace the question mark?

251 Twelve runners in a marathon were lined up as follows.

8	5	4	46	52	61
7	6	9	94	63	?

What number should the 12th runner have?

252 What number is missing?

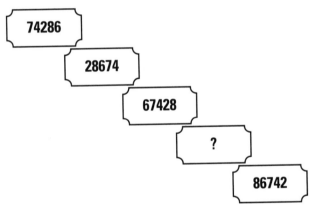

74286

28674

67428

?

86742

253 Multiply the highest prime number by the lowest even number and subtract the result from the sum total of the numbers remaining.

14 20 13 7 16 11 3 10 17 18 8 12 5 6

254 What is **X**?

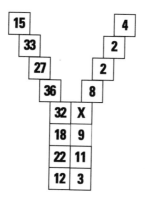

255 Arrange these patterns into four pairs.

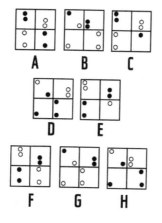

A   B   C

D   E

F   G   H

256 Each symbol stands for a different number. In order to reach the correct total at the end of each row and column, what is the value of the circle, cross, pentagon, square, and star?

Circle =
Cross =
Pentagon =
Square =
Star =

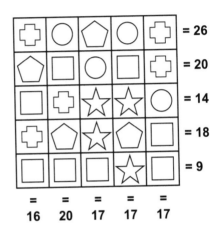

257 What number should replace the question mark?

16		14
	10	
10		4

37		15
	6	
8		10

29		3
	?	
18		10

258 Sudoku

	9			3		6		
								4
		1	5		2			
5		3						8
				4				
6						7		2
			9		7	5		
8								
		4		1			3	

259 What number should replace the question mark?

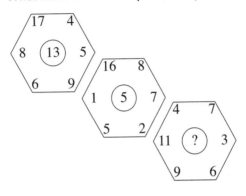

260 I went into a furniture shop in order to buy a picture. The salesman told me, "The picture is five times the cost of that vase; the chair is 30 times the cost of the vase; the table is 4 times the cost of the chair; you can buy the lot for $312."

What was the price of the picture?

261 Which is the odd number out?

49   91   37

112   133   154

262 Which number completes this sequence?

3   8   18   38   ?

263 The invoice read "Wine" " – 67.9 – " The first and last digits were missing. There were 72 bottles.

How much did each cost? (Each bottle cost the same).

264 What number should replace the question mark?

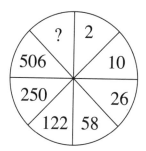

265 Give values for **X** and **Y**.

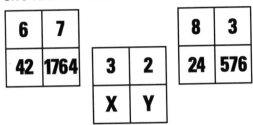

6	7
42	1764

3	2
X	Y

8	3
24	576

266 Mrs. Black, Mrs. Red, and Mrs. Brown met in the hairdresser's. One of them said, "I have black hair, and you two have red hair and brown hair, but none of us has the hair color that matches her name."

Mrs. Brown responded, "You are quite right."

What color is Mrs. Red's hair?

267 What should replace the question marks?

A	5	D	11	G	17	J
						23
						M
?	?	Y	47	V	41	S	35	P	29

7

268 Kakuro

269 What are the two missing digits?

1 1 1 3 1 2 1 6 1 3
1 9 1 4 2 2 1 – 2 –

270 What numbers are represented by A, B, and C?

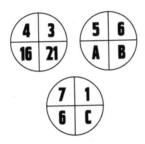

271 What numbers should replace the question marks?

21	23	22	25	27	26
34	35	33	30	31	29
37	39	38	?	43	42
50	51	49	?	47	45
53	55	54	57	59	58
66	67	65	62	63	61

272 Many people are aware that when the sums of the alternate digits of a number are equal, that number is always divisible by 11 exactly, for example, the number 3685 is divisible by 11 exactly because:

$$3 + 8 = 6 + 5$$

It, therefore, follows that if the first three digits of a number are, for example, 256, then the addition of a 3 to the end of that number—2563—will make it divisible by 11 because 2 + 6 = 5 + 3.

However, it does not necessarily follow that every number which is divisible by 11 exactly has the sums of its alternate digits equal. As an example, take the number 987652413. This number is exactly divisible by 11, even though its alternate digits are unequal.

There is, however, a further simple rule which will show that this number is divisible by 11 exactly, without the use of multiplication or division.

Can you determine what this simple rule is?

273 Can you place the hexagons into the grid, so that where any hexagon touches another along a straight line, the contents of both triangles are the same? No rotation of any hexagon is allowed!

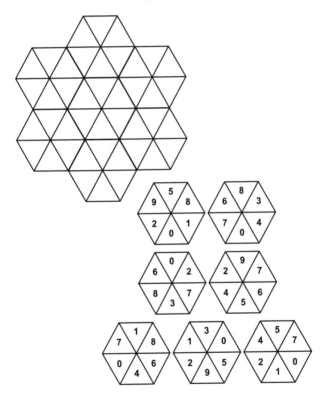

274 Kakuro

275 Sudoku

4								
5	2	8		3				
				1		2		
			2				6	
3				4				5
	9				7			
	7		6					
				5		4	7	8
								9

276 Kakuro

277 Supply the missing number:

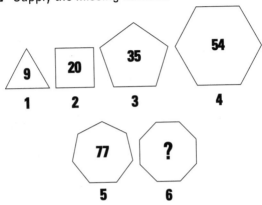

1. 9
2. 20
3. 35
4. 54
5. 77
6. ?

278 Find the starting square and follow the directions to arrive on the square marked T. Every square must be visited once only.

1N, 3E means 1 North, 3 East.

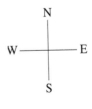

2S 2E	2E 3S	2W 1S	3W
3E 1S	1E 2S	1W 2S	2S 3W
2N 3E	1N 2E	T	3W
1E 2N	1E 3N	1W 3N	2N 1W

Solutions

1 Two revolutions clockwise.
C (24 teeth) rotates 4 revolutions. Therefore D also rotates 4 revolutions. Pulley B has twice the circumference of pulley D and so will rotate 2 revolutions. A rotates clockwise, so B rotates counterclockwise and C rotates clockwise. C does not change the direction of D, so D and E also rotate clockwise.

2 A 4, B 4
When correctly spaced they are:
A 4   8   16   32   64   128
B 19   38   76   152   304

3 808
Multiply each pair of numbers on the top row to get the three pairs of numbers on the second row, then multiply the second row pairs to get the third row, etc.

4 ANN
Give each letter a number according to its position in the alphabet.
TED = 20 + 5 + 4 (29)
ANN = 1 + 14 + 14 (29)
(George and Mary each add to 57)

5 B
A contains 7 triangles **B** contains 11 triangles
C contains 10 triangles **D** contains 6 triangles

6 5
The numbers are the alphabetical positions of the letters, spelling FACADE: 6-F; 1-A; 3-C; 1-A; 4-D; 5-E.

7 Alan 16, Bertie 27, Charlie 39

8 Turn the numbers upside down.

$$\begin{array}{r} 96 \\ 88 \\ 99 \\ \underline{11} \\ \underline{294} \end{array}$$

9 B and C
They become:
```
5 4 1
3 1 6
2 5 3
```

10 55706065
In the first line multiply the digits outside the brackets by 2 in this order: extreme left, extreme right, second left, and first right. In the second line multiply by 3, and in the third line by 4, following the same procedure. Therefore in the fourth line multiply by 5 and follow the same procedure.

11 3

So that all lines across and down total 10.

12 Mary 44, Sally 66, Frank 99.

13 913

The figures 3462891 are being repeated in the same order.

14 36 minutes

15 D

D adds up to 36. The others add up to 33.

16 4½"

17

5	6	7	3	4	8	2	1	9
4	2	3	9	1	5	8	7	6
1	9	8	7	2	6	3	5	4
9	4	1	5	7	2	6	3	8
7	5	6	8	3	4	1	9	2
3	8	2	6	9	1	5	4	7
2	7	5	4	8	3	9	6	1
8	3	4	1	6	9	7	2	5
6	1	9	2	5	7	4	8	3

18 128

The consecutive numbers are: 9, 10, 11; 17, 18; 20, 21, and 22.

19 4
Looking across and down the middle number is the sum of the two other numbers either left or right or above and below, divided by 2.

20 **A** + ÷, **B** × ÷ or ÷ × or − + or + −, **C** × −, **D** × ×

21 18
The two odd numbers are subtracted from the even number in each square.

22 2 8 9 4
The two numbers on the right of the previous brackets are the numbers on the left inside the brackets; the numbers on the left of the previous brackets are the numbers on the right inside the brackets.

23 10—Three-eighths of 168 = 63; five-ninths of 63 = 35; two-sevenths of 35 = 10.

24 A=137, B=19, C=52, D=102, E=45, F=156, G=71, H=154, I=147, J=227, K=225, L=301, M=452, N=526, O=978.

25 8
Add the numbers in the right and left squares to obtain the numbers in the middle square.

26

7	9		1	2	7			2	1
1	2		5	8	9			6	2
9	8	1	4	2		2	8	9	7	3
	4	9				9	7		
5	9		1	2	4	6	3		9	7
1	3	9		1	6	9		4	6	2
	1	8	7	9		1	4	3	2
	6	1				8	1		
	1	5	3	2		8	9	5	7
9	2	7		6	8	9		2	3	9
8	4		4	1	3	2	8		1	5
	3	8				9	6		
8	7	1	9	5		4	5	1	7	9
9	3		1	4	2			9	8
7	1		3	9	8			2	6

27 50

6 x 15 = 90, 7 x 18 = 126, 7 x 20 = 140

28 87

The numbers are considered as moving clockwise in each successive large square. In each case they add up to 100:

14 – 50 – 8 – 28

19 – 41 – 30 – 10

22 – 22 – 22 – 34

8 – 1 – 4 – 87 (X)

29 6380

The numbers inside the brackets are the squares of the numbers outside the brackets with 1 deducted. Alternatively, multiply 2, 4, 6, and 8 by 4, 6, 8, and 10

respectively, and put the number at the end of the
figure in the brackets, and multiply 3, 5, 7, and 9 by 1,
3, 5, and 7 respectively and put these numbers first.

30 52
$6 \times 5 = 30 - 7 = 23$
$2 \times 8 = 16 - 9 = 7$
$14 \times 2 = 28 - 6 = 22$
$8 \times 7 = 56 - 4 = 52$

31 12

	1st face	2nd face	3rd face
1st move	1	2	6
2nd move	4	3	2
3rd move	6	5	1

32 23

33 133

34

1	3	4	9	7	8	6	5	2
5	8	7	2	1	6	9	4	3
6	9	2	5	3	4	8	1	7
3	2	8	6	5	1	7	9	4
7	5	6	3	4	9	1	2	8
9	4	1	8	2	7	5	3	6
4	7	9	1	8	2	3	6	5
2	1	3	7	6	5	4	8	9
8	6	5	4	9	3	2	7	1

35 36

The scores are: 1, 7, 1, 7, 1, 2, 1, 5, 1, 4, 1, 4, and 1.

36 **C** 2 7 1 0 9 8 6

37 100

$$6 \times 7 = 42$$
$$12 \times 3 = 36$$
$$\underline{11}$$
$$89$$

$$8 \times 2 = 16$$
$$5 \times 21 = 105$$
$$\underline{2}$$
$$123$$

$$6 \times 7 = 42$$
$$14 \times 4 = 56$$
$$\underline{2}$$
$$100$$

38 E

All the others contain three consecutive digits.

39

```
4 8 | 6 4 | 7 9 | 7 4
2 1 | 9 6 | 1 8 | 5 2
1 6 2 | 1 4 5 | 8 9 6
      3 6 2 9 | 3 7 8 9
7 1 | 7 3 | 5 1 6
8 2 1 5 | 5 9 | 2 3 1
9 8 4 | 5 2 4 1 | 9 5
      3 9 7 | 8 2 1
8 1 | 2 1 3 7 | 6 9 7
9 4 1 | 2 6 | 5 2 3 1
      8 5 3 | 1 3 | 8 9
8 4 9 7 | 9 7 8 1
2 1 4 | 6 7 2 | 5 8 9
1 3 | 9 5 | 3 5 | 9 7
4 2 | 4 3 | 4 6 | 2 1
```

40 2.5 minutes

41 16

42 1½

$$\frac{9}{72} \div \frac{36}{144} \div \frac{12}{36} =$$

$$\frac{1}{8} \div \frac{1}{4} \div \frac{1}{3} =$$

$$\frac{1}{8} \times \frac{4}{1} \times \frac{3}{1} = \frac{12}{8} = 1½$$

43 106
$5 \times 2, 1 \times 6$

44 41
$4 \times 8 + 9$

45

8	5	2	4	3	7	1	9	6
6	3	1	9	2	8	7	4	5
4	7	9	1	5	6	3	2	8
1	4	7	8	6	3	2	5	9
5	6	8	2	7	9	4	1	3
2	9	3	5	4	1	6	8	7
9	2	6	3	8	4	5	7	1
3	1	4	7	9	5	8	6	2
7	8	5	6	1	2	9	3	4

46 2573

In all the other numbers, multiply the first and last digits to obtain the middle two.

47 14

48 $\dfrac{1}{13}$ x $\dfrac{1}{12}$ x $\dfrac{1}{11}$ x $\dfrac{1}{10}$ = $\dfrac{1}{17160}$

or
17159 to 1

49 D = DIAMOND   H = 11   C = 8   D = 5   S = 1

50 A 4, **B** 8

51 14
(17 + 11 + 12) − (14 + 19) = 7
(18 + 16 + 15) − (6 + 5) = 38
(19 + 16 + 2) − (15 + 8) = 14

52 3

53

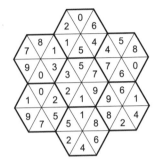

54 17 + 6 + 5 + 9 − (11 + 2 + 4 + 8) = 12

55 20 and 37 or 3
Opposite segments add up to 27.
Opposite segments are subtracted = 17.

56 30 and 11
There are two interwoven sequences: starting from
the first 4, the sequence progresses +5, +6, +7, +8;
then starting at the 1, the sequence progresses +1,
+2, +3, +4.

57

58 A is 3, B is 7, C is 4.

There are several pointers to the solution; for example, in the last vertical column A cannot be 5, 6, 7, 8, or 9.

59

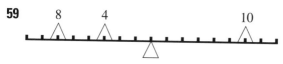

3 x 4 = 12   6 x 10 = 60
8 x 6 = <u>48</u>
         60

60 2, 4, 8, 16, 32, and 64

61 99

Add the first digit of the previous number, then the second digit, and so on.

62 1
The numbers reduce by 17, 34, 68, 136, 272, and 544, thus reducing the previous number (545) to 1.

63 46923
Reverse all but the last two digits of the previous number, then add the last two digits.

64 7
Start at 11 and move clockwise. Opposite segments as indicated in the diagram below are plus 1, then plus 2, etc.

17	14	5	16
11			1
7			12
21	9	17	19

65 There are two answers.
Either 239 cats killed 4,649 rats (A) or 4,649 cats killed 239 rats (B). (A) is the most likely answer.

66 6859
They are cube numbers:

16^3	17^3	18^3	19^3
4096	4913	5832	6859

67 A 15 B 6 C 3 D 1

68 $61

69 5
Taking pairs of dominoes, one from the extreme left

of the row and one from the extreme right of the row, both show the same point total. Repeat this sequence, working toward the center.

70 The minute hand moves forward by 11 minutes and the hour hand moves back by 3 hours each time.

71 The pentagon has the greatest number by 180º. Diamond 360º, double triangle 360º, pentagon 540º.

72

73

6	8	5	2	4	7	3	9	1
2	1	3	5	8	9	7	6	4
9	4	7	3	1	6	2	8	5
8	2	4	9	7	5	6	1	3
5	7	9	6	3	1	8	4	2
1	3	6	8	2	4	9	5	7
7	6	8	1	5	2	4	3	9
3	5	2	4	9	8	1	7	6
4	9	1	7	6	3	5	2	8

74 50

Think of the star as being made of two superimposed triangles, the numbers in the three angles of each totaling the number in the center.

75 32

$(9 + 8 + 13 + 6 + 10) - (6 + 7 + 1 + 8 + 4) = 20$
$(11 + 12 + 6 + 7 + 8) - (5 + 2 + 4 + 1 + 2) = 30$
$(17 + 14 + 12 + 9 + 7) - (11 + 7 + 3 + 2 + 4) = 32$

76 108

Three-fifths of 1215 = 729; one-third of 729 = 243; four-ninths of 243 = 108.

77

9	4	1	3	8	5	6	7	2
6	3	7	4	9	2	1	5	8
8	2	5	1	7	6	3	4	9
5	1	3	6	2	7	9	8	4
2	8	9	5	3	4	7	1	6
4	7	6	9	1	8	5	2	3
1	5	4	8	6	9	2	3	7
7	6	8	2	5	3	4	9	1
3	9	2	7	4	1	8	6	5

78 156

$(12 \times 8) + (6 \times 14) - (2 + 8 + 10 + 4)$

79 B. 177

80 17

81 E = 36
Add the number of sides then multiply by 3.

82 38
(5 x 4) + (10 + 8)=38

83 1 hour
40 miles at 40 mph = 1 hour;
60 miles at 60 mph = 1 hour.

84 15
All the others are prime numbers.

85 The clock moves back 4 hours 41 minutes, forward 1 hour 44 minutes, back 4 hours 41 minutes, and forward 1 hour 44 minutes.

86 152

87

88

14	**21**	10	23	14	14
25	26	18	21	**2**	4
22	9	**6**	28	21	10
12	9	30	4	17	24
9	8	6	11	32	**30**
14	23	26	**9**	10	14

89 110 miles (the odometer read 16061)

90 6, 3, 18
A plus E = B,
A plus B = D,
D divided by E = C

91 729

Squares 13–499	16, 25, 36, 49, 64, 81, 100, 121, 144, 169, 196, 225, 256, 289, 324, 361, 400, 441, 484
Squares 500–1300	529, 576, 625, 676, 729, 784, 841, 900, 961, 1024, 1089, 1156, 1225, 1296
Cubes 13–499	27, 64, 125, 216, 343
Cubes 500–1300	512, 729, 1000
Both	64, 729

Possible true answers:
Questions 1 and 2 – No
Questions 1 and 3 – No
Questions 2 and 3 – Yes, over 500 there is a cube
and a square—729

92 4
All lines across total 8.

93 6:50

94 F.
In the others, the middle three digits add up to 10.

95 8¹⁄₆ cigarettes

96 −24
Deduct 4, 8, 16, 32, and 64 (i.e., doubling the amount
deducted each time).

97

8	9	1	2	6	5	3	4	7
5	3	7	9	4	1	8	6	2
4	6	2	8	7	3	5	1	9
1	8	5	3	2	7	6	9	4
2	7	3	6	9	4	1	5	8
6	4	9	5	1	8	2	7	3
7	1	6	4	8	2	9	3	5
9	5	8	7	3	6	4	2	1
3	2	4	1	5	9	7	8	6

98 B.
In lines across multiply the number of circles to obtain the number in the third square. In lines down divide.

99 $18^{5}/_{8}$
There are 2 series.
16, $16^{7}/_{8}$, $17^{3}/_{4}$, $18^{5}/_{8}$
(+ $^{7}/_{8}$ and $- ^{3}/_{4}$)
21, $20^{1}/_{4}$, $19^{1}/_{2}$

100 5
$(7 + 2 + 4) - (6 + 5) = 2$
$(9 + 1 + 7) - (2 + 2) = 13$
$(11 + 4 + 2) - (5 + 2) = 10$

101 4
The numbers are the number of letters in each word of the question.

102 $25' \times 25'$
$15' \times 15'$

103 21
The numbers increase by 3, 4, 5, 6, and 7.

104 X = 129 Y = 39
In the outer ring, moving clockwise, each number is doubled and 1 subtracted from the result.

In the inner ring, moving clockwise, each number is doubled and 1 added to the result.

105 12

106 52 × 51 × 50 × 49 = 6,497,400

107 81

108 A

With the exception of the digits in A, which add up to 13, the digits in all other dates add up to 12.

109

110 630

Multiply by three quarters, one half, one quarter and repeat.

111 2
Opposite numbers total 11.

112 X is 9; Y is 15.
There are two separate series. Starting with the first number and taking the others alternately: 1 3 5 7 9
Starting with the second number and proceeding in the same way: 3 6 9 12 15

113 Clocks gain 2 hours 19 minutes, 2 hours 29 minutes, 2 hours 39 minutes, and 2 hours 49 minutes.

114 Jack

115 90°F

116 B
Starting at the top left number and working clockwise, subtract the next number, add the next number, and continue likewise until you arrive at 20 in the center.

117

5	4	8	2	6	3	7	1	9
7	3	2	5	1	9	8	6	4
6	9	1	4	7	8	3	5	2
2	8	6	1	4	5	9	3	7
9	7	4	6	3	2	5	8	1
1	5	3	9	8	7	2	4	6
4	2	7	3	5	1	6	9	8
8	1	5	7	9	6	4	2	3
3	6	9	8	2	4	1	7	5

118 4

$A + D = B + E + C$

119 207

$3^2, + 4^2, + 5^2, + 6^2, + 7^2$

120 2415

121 42

122 59

Proceeding from top to bottom along the rows from left to right, add the two previous numbers and add 1, then add the two previous numbers and subtract 1, and so forth, adding 1 and subtracting 1 alternately. Thus the two numbers previous to the blank square are 22 and 38. These are added together, giving 60, and 1 subtracted from the total.

123 D

D equals 3; all the others equal 4

124 15

$26 - 10 = 16$	$14 - 7 = 7$	$21 - 9 = 12$	$17 - 10 = 7$
$31 - \ 9 = \underline{22}$	$12 - 5 = \underline{7}$	$11 - 2 = \underline{\ 9}$	$9 - \ 1 = \underline{8}$
38	14	21	15

125 A = 98   B = 126

In the first row the numbers outside the brackets

are divided by 12 and the results placed inside the
brackets; in the second row they are divided by
13; thus, in the third row the numbers inside the
brackets are multiplied by 14 to obtain A and B.

126 16

7+6=13	2+16=18	17+6=23
12+2=14	4+15=19	8+16=24
7+8=15	10+10=20	13+12=25
3+13=16	14+7=21	10+16=26
5+12=17	14+8=22	13+14=27

127 13

128 102 and 106
The sequence progresses:
x2, +1, x2, +2, x2, +3, x2, and +4.

129 29
The diagram should contain the 6th to the 13th prime
numbers.

130 1000
The top circle contains the squares of 6, 7, 8, 9, and
10: 36, 49, 64, 81, and 100.
The bottom circle contains the cubes of 6, 7, 8, 9,
and 10: 216, 343, 512, 729, and 1000.

131 63

132 Clocks gain 3 hours 33 minutes, 2 hours 33 minutes, 1 hour 33 minutes, and finally 33 minutes each time.

133 86
Add five straight down; add ten sideways; add fifteen diagonally.

134 48
The figures in the squares are non-prime numbers between 38 and 48.

135 8
Starting with the two segments above **X**, the sum of each set of two segments in the upper semicircle is the same as their opposing pair in the lower semicircle.

136

137 The hour hand gains 2, 4, 6, and 8
hours; and the minute hand loses 8, 6, 4,
and 2 minutes each time.

138 140
Starting with 3 in the upper half, the
number in the opposite segment multiplies it by 2.
The next number (7) is multiplied by 3; then by 4, and
so on. Therefore 20 is multiplied by 7 to give 140.

139 2
Each side of the triangle contains the numbers 1–9.

140 13 seats
Thirty-seven people each paid $51.

141 16
Giving vowels a value of 1 and consonants a value of
3 means ALSATIAN = 16

142 10
There are eight groups of three numbers around the
diamond totaling 15: 10 + 3 + 2 = 15; 8 + 2 + 5 = 15 etc.

143 29
The odd numbers in A total 39; the even numbers
in B total 40. From this combined total of 79 is
subtracted 50—the total of the prime numbers in C.

144 3

145 20
$(7 + 26 + 17) - (8 + 12 + 10) = 20$

146

7	9	1	8	6	2	5	3	4
4	5	6	1	3	7	2	8	9
8	2	3	4	9	5	7	1	6
5	3	8	2	7	6	4	9	1
6	4	7	9	5	1	3	2	8
2	1	9	3	8	4	6	5	7
3	7	2	6	1	9	8	4	5
1	6	4	5	2	8	9	7	3
9	8	5	7	4	3	1	6	2

147 8 kg

Left	Right
8 kg × 5 = 40	6 kg × 4 = 24
4 kg × 2 = 8	8 kg × 3 = 24
48	48

148 8
Numbers in the same shape of geometric figure all total 11.

149 23
Add 2 to the first 2 numbers, then 3 to the next 3 numbers, etc.

150 4, 4, 2, 2

151

152

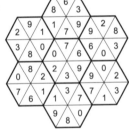

153

5

4

6

There are three sequences: 1,2,3,4,5 alternating top second; 0,1,2,3,4 alternating second third; and 2,3,4,5,6 alternating third first.

154 $\dfrac{46}{27} \div \dfrac{92}{9}$

$$\dfrac{46}{27} \times \dfrac{9}{92} = \dfrac{414}{2484} = \dfrac{1}{6}$$

155 A 36   D 35
       B 4   E 24
       C 9

156 The value of the central letter is the total value of the letters in the top right, top left, and bottom right squares, minus the value of the letter in the bottom left square. Thus the missing value is 9, so the missing letter is I.

157 48
$(6 + 7) \times (5 - 2) = 39$
$(8 + 6) \times (4 - 1) = 42$
$(10 + 2) \times (6 - 2) = 48$

158 2, 3, 5, 8

159 89
Moving diagonally left to right from top to bottom, each number decreases by the same amount as the number before.

160 $6/100 \times 5/99 = 1/330$

161 8%
$81 + 82 + 77 + 68 = 308$
Among 100 pupils, this gives 3 losses each, and 4
losses to 8 pupils.

162

8	6	5	4	1	2	7	9	3
3	9	7	6	5	8	2	4	1
1	2	4	7	3	9	5	8	6
9	3	2	1	7	4	6	5	8
7	4	6	8	9	5	1	3	2
5	1	8	3	2	6	4	7	9
2	8	9	5	4	1	3	6	7
6	5	3	2	8	7	9	1	4
4	7	1	9	6	3	8	2	5

163 7
Opposite numbers are multiplied and then the totals
are added.

$$6 \times 4 = 24$$
$$7 \times 3 = 21$$
$$21 \times 9 = \underline{189}$$
$$234$$

$$11 \times 9 = 99$$
$$2 \times 7 = 14$$
$$8 \times 8 = \underline{64}$$
$$177$$

$$31 \times 6 = 186$$
$$5 \times 14 = 70$$
$$8 \times (7) = \underline{56}$$
$$312$$

164 X is 108; Y is 48.

There are three series, taking every third term:

3	6	12	24	48	(Y multiply by 2)
7	21	84	420		(multiply by 3, 4, and 5)
4	12	36	108		(X multiply by 3)

165 X is 7; Y is 9.

Although this can be solved by elimination, it can also be solved by algebra: from the bottom line:

$$y = 2 + x$$

substituting this in the first line:

$$2x - (2 + x) = 5$$

hence:

$$2x - 2 - x = 5;$$

or

$$x - 2 = 5,$$

therefore

$$x = 7$$

substituting this in the second line:

$$7 + y = 16$$

therefore:

$$y = 9$$

166 A) 1998 lbs   C) Not possible
   B) 666 lbs   D) Not possible

167 7 kg

Left	Right
6 kg × 4 = 24	7 kg × 4 = 28
8 kg × 2 = <u>16</u>	6 kg × 2 = <u>12</u>
40	40

168 269, since 269 x 2 = 538

169 21 + 6 − 11 x 5 = 80

170 X is 4½ or 4.5; Y is 112.
Halve the terms alternately from the first term: 72 36
18 9 4½ or 4.5 (X). Double the terms alternately from
the second term:
7 14 28 56 112 (Y).

171 George 10, Henry 12, Malcolm 9

172 35 (5 × 7)

173 2 new stations; 11 existing stations

174 GC, 73
The numbers in the middle indicate the position
of the letters on the left from the beginning of the
alphabet, and the position of the letters on the right
from the end.

175 1.75

There are two alternate sequences: + 1.25 and − 2.75.

176

177 Analyze the statements.

Hole No.	A	B	C	D	E
1	✓		✓	✓	✓
2					✓
3	✓				✓
4			✓	✓	
5	✓				✓
6				✓	✓
7	✓		✓		✓
8				✓	✓

9	✓			✓	
10		✓		✓	✓
11	✓		✓		✓
12		✓		✓	✓
13	✓				✓
14		✓		✓	✓
15	✓			✓	✓
16		✓		✓	
17	✓		✓		✓
18		✓		✓	✓

Only one check means a true statement.
Hole No. 2

178 17
The number in each inner segment is the sum of the digits in the opposite outer segment, i.e., 9 + 8 = 17.

179

4	6	8
7	T	2
1	3	5

180 16

The spots on two of the dominoes total 11, not 12.

181 14

182 D

Add the numbers and then add the remaining digits:
A – total of numbers is 25, 2 plus 5 = 7;
B – total of numbers is 34, 3 plus 4 = 7;
C – total of the numbers is 61, 6 plus 1 = 7;
D – total of the numbers is 26, 2 plus 6 = 8.

183 12

The series must be read backwards and spaced correctly: 1 2 3 4 5 6 7 8 9 10 11 12 (X).

184

$$\frac{3}{4} \times \frac{32}{27} = \frac{96}{108} = \frac{8}{9}$$

185 A

Gear A has 20 teeth. Gear C has 10 teeth. Therefore the ratio between them is exactly 2:1, which is obtained by dividing the larger by the smaller. In other words, gear A will make two revolutions while gear C makes one. The number of teeth on the intermediate gear does not in any way alter the ratio between the other two.

186 44
$(9 \times 5) - (6 - 4)$
$(8 \times 7) - (9 - 3)$
$(7 \times 7) - (10 - 5)$

187 88 years

188

6	8	7	1	9	4	2	3	5
2	9	5	3	8	7	4	1	6
4	3	1	2	5	6	9	8	7
7	6	8	9	4	3	5	2	1
1	4	9	6	2	5	3	7	8
3	5	2	8	7	1	6	4	9
8	7	4	5	3	9	1	6	2
5	2	6	4	1	8	7	9	3
9	1	3	7	6	2	8	5	4

189 6
$(5 \times 6 \times 7) \div (3 + 7) = 21$
$(4 \times 9 \times 2) \div (4 + 4) = 9$
$(6 \times 1 \times 9) \div (4 + 5) = 6$

190 2
$(17+8+9) - (14+11+3) = 6$
$(21+2+9) - (1+17+3) = 11$
$(6+22+4) - (1+17+12) = 2$

191 96 and 121
In the top row the numbers are square numbers (3, 5, 7, and 9) except 96; in the bottom row the numbers

are even numbers (8, 12, 18, and 14) except 121
(which is the square of 11).

192 6
The player holds 1 club, 2 hearts, and 4 diamonds.
As he holds 13 cards (or seven black cards), it
follows that there must be 6 spades.

193 1
Spaced correctly, the series becomes 13 15 17 19
2(1).

194 447
The square numbers are: 16 (4 squared), 225 (15
squared), 81 (9 squared), and 64 (8 squared), which
equal 386. The prime numbers are: 7, 31, and 23,
which equal 61. 386 + 61 = 447

195 2 kg

Left	Right
6 kg x 4 = 24	12 kg x 3 = 36
10 kg x 2 = 20	2 kg x 4 = 8
44	44

196 X = 2, Y = 4
3x2=6, 6x6=36
1x4=4, 4x4=16
1x2=2, 2x2=4

The lower left hand number is the product of the two top numbers; the bottom right hand number is the square of the bottom left hand number.

197 A
Assign a number to each letter according to its place in the alphabet, so E=5, F=6, M=13, W=23, and C=3, making a total of 50. The total in the center is 51, so the missing letter is A (=1).

198 X is 21; Y is 24; and Z is 17.

There are three separate series. Start with the first term and take every third term thereafter:
76 65 54 43 32
As they reduce by 11 each time, the next term, X, must be 21.

199 The southbound train ran one minute after the northbound train.

200 The hour hand alternately gains 3 and 7 hours and the minute hand alternately loses 7 and 3 minutes each time.

201

202 6 hours, 19 minutes, 52 seconds

The present time shown is 2 hours, 50 minutes, 6 seconds. Ignoring the seconds, the time in 3½ hours will be 6.20. In the meantime, the second hand will have lost 14 seconds. Instead of showing six seconds AFTER the hour it will show eight seconds BEFORE the hour—that is, 52 seconds. This means that the minute hand will not have reached the 20-minute mark, but will have passed the 19-minute mark.

203 117

204 ³⁄₁₀ x ²⁄₉ = ⁶⁄₉₀ = ¹⁄₁₅

205 X is 4.
Square the middle number in each horizontal row

and subtract the left-hand number to give the right-hand number. So, in the bottom row:
3 squared is 9; subtract 5.

206 7
The moves result as follows:

	A	B
1st move	7	10
2nd move	11	4
3rd move	3	10
4th move	7	4
5th move	11	10
6th move	3	4 (Total: 7)

207 2
Starting at 7 and working clockwise, two adjacent numbers in the top semicircle are added. In the opposite segments are factors of that total:

7 + 8 = 15; 3 × 5 = 15
3 + 5 = 8; 2 × 4 = 8
9 + 9 = 18; 9 × 2 = 18

Hence:
8 + 4 = 12; 6 × 2 = 12

208

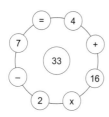

209 $6^3 \div 36 = 6$

210 13
The totals of the columns are: 4 9 16 25 36 49
In other words, 2 squared, 3 squared, 4 squared, etc.

211

2	4	1	7	5	3	6	8	9
6	3	5	8	9	4	2	7	1
8	7	9	2	1	6	3	5	4
7	1	6	4	3	8	5	9	2
5	9	2	1	6	7	8	4	3
4	8	3	9	2	5	7	1	6
1	5	4	3	8	2	9	6	7
3	6	7	5	4	9	1	2	8
9	2	8	6	7	1	4	3	5

212 Black 2, Green 3, Brown 4, Smith 5
120 is made up of $2 \times 3 \times 4 \times 5$.

213 24 minutes

214 Bill 52, Ben 39

215 17
The numbers in each vertical column total 98.

216 4
(4) × 19 = 76
3 × 27 = 81
7 × 13 = 91

217 21 15
Each number is calculated using the two numbers below. In rows 2 and 4, take the difference of the two numbers below; in rows 3 and 5 add.

218 35
There are 2 series of numbers:
In the first series add 6 (17 + 6 = 23).
In the second series subtract 6 (35 − 6) = 29.

219 28

220 9

221 24
6 x 8 = 48 ÷ 2 = 24

222

223 13

224 14

225 43¾
Each figure is multiplied by 2½.

226 36
The number in the lowest left box is the cube and
the number in the lowest right box is the square of
the number in the top box.

227 5 kilograms

1 kilo	weight available
2 kilos	3 kg on one side; 1 kg on the other side
3 kilos	weight available
4 kilos	3 kg and 1 kg on one side

5 kilos	not possible
6 kilos	3 kg and 1 kg on one side; 10 kg on the other side
7 kilos	3 kg on one side; 10 kg on the other side
8 kilos	3 kg on one side;10 kg and 1 kg on the other side
9 kilos	1 kg on one side; 10 kg on the other side
10 kilos	weight available
11 kilos	10 kg and 1 kg on one side
12 kilos	10 kg and 3 kg on one side; 1 kg on the other side
13 kilos	10 kg and 3 kg on one side
14 kilos	10 kg, 3 kg and 1 kg on one side.

228

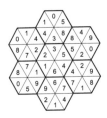

229 2
$54 + 16 = 70 \div (18 + 17) = 2$
$90 + 9 = 99 \div (19 + 14) = 3$
$55 + 35 = 90 \div (26 + 19) = 2$

230 $\frac{1}{36}$

231 12

In the first hexagon opposite numbers add up to 36. In the second hexagon opposite numbers add up to 43. In the third hexagon opposite numbers add up to 32.

232 $6 \times 5 = 30$

233

5	7	4	6	1	3	8	9	2
3	6	2	8	4	9	5	1	7
1	8	9	7	2	5	3	4	6
8	4	6	3	7	1	2	5	9
7	3	5	2	9	8	4	6	1
2	9	1	5	6	4	7	3	8
4	1	8	9	5	7	6	2	3
6	5	7	1	3	2	9	8	4
9	2	3	4	8	6	1	7	5

234 23

There are two series:
(+3)   17, 20, 23, 26
(−6)   41, 35, 29, 23

235 $(21 \times 14) - 3 - 3 = 288$

236 2

Start at the top and then move right to left along the second row, then back left to right along the third row etc., repeating the numbers 36942.

237

9 8		4 9		7 1		3 9
1 2		1 5		9 3		2 5
3 1 5		1 5		2 7 1 4
	6 9		6 8		9 6 8
7 3 1 2		3 1 2 4	
9 1		2 8		5 8 3 9
8 4 6 7 5 9 3		8 5
	8 6 9		5 9 8	
9 7		6 3 1 5 4 8 2
8 3 4 1		1 2		7 1
	9 7 8 6		8 9 6 4
5 3 1		3 2		1 2	
9 5 8 2		5 4		3 9 7
7 1		1 6		8 3		8 2
8 2		5 9		9 1		3 1

238 222

In each pair of circles the sum of the numbers in the second circle should be 80 less than the sum of the numbers in the first circle. In the last pair the sum of the numbers in the first circle is 1546, so X must be 222 to bring the sum of the numbers in the second circle to 1466.

239 3¼

There are two series.

The first series is: + 1¼ (9 + 1¼ = 10¼).

The second series is – 1¼ (7 – 1¼ = 5¾).

240 25

241

2	3	8	6	7	5	1	4	9
9	1	6	3	8	4	5	7	2
5	4	7	9	1	2	3	6	8
4	8	9	5	3	6	7	2	1
1	2	5	8	9	7	6	3	4
7	6	3	4	2	1	8	9	5
6	9	2	7	5	8	4	1	3
8	7	1	2	4	3	9	5	6
3	5	4	1	6	9	2	8	7

242

243 22

There are two series:

(+6)   7-13-19-25
(+7)   8-15-22-29

244 12

245 1 minute

$(0.5 + 0.25) \times \dfrac{80}{60}$

246 $8^2 + 7^2 + 6^2 + 5^2 + 4^2 + 3^2 + 2^2 + 1^2 = 204$

247 121

$72 - 61 = 11$; $11 \times 11 = 121$

248 Blue

The numbered colored shirts coincide with the colors of the rainbow; blue is the fifth color of the rainbow.

249 86

Each number on the right is the digits of the number on the left, reversed, then minus one.

250 9 Diamonds

Every row and column contains one of each suit, so the missing card is a diamond. In each row, subtract the sum of the black cards from the sum of the red cards to give the value of the Heart on the right hand side. King=13, Queen=12, Jack=11.

251 18

$8 \times 8 = 64$ Reversed = 46 $7 \times 7 = 49$ Reversed = 94

$5 \times 5 = 25$ Reversed = 52 $6 \times 6 = 36$ Reversed = 63

$4 \times 4 = 16$ Reversed = 61 $9 \times 9 = 81$ Reversed = 18

252 42867
Each number is the last three digits of the number above followed by the first two digits.

253 35
The highest prime number is 17, and the lowest even number is 6. The remaining numbers add to 137.

254 4
The top left-hand number is the result of adding the two bottom numbers. The top right-hand number is the result of dividing the bottom two numbers. If this procedure is followed throughout, **X** must be 4, to make the top horizontal pair 36.

255 AF, BH, CE, DG

256 Circle = 7, cross = 3, pentagon = 6, square = 2, star = 1

257 5
$16 + 14 + 10 \div 4 = 10$
$37 + 15 + 8 \div 10 = 6$
$29 + 3 + 18 \div 10 = 5$

258

7	9	2	1	3	4	6	8	5
3	6	5	8	7	9	1	2	4
4	8	1	5	6	2	9	7	3
5	7	3	6	2	1	4	9	8
1	2	9	7	4	8	3	5	6
6	4	8	3	9	5	7	1	2
2	3	6	9	8	7	5	4	1
8	1	7	4	5	3	2	6	9
9	5	4	2	1	6	8	3	7

259 8
$(17 + 8 + 6) - (4 + 5 + 9) = 13$
$(16 + 1 + 5) - (8 + 7 + 2) = 5$
$(4 + 11 + 9) - (7 + 3 + 6) = 8$

260 $10
Vase $2; Chair $60; Table $240

261 37
All the others are divisible by 7.

262 78
Starting on the left, double each number and add 2.

263 72 at $5.11 each = $367.92

264 1018
Moving clockwise, double the previous number and add 6.

265 X = 6; Y = 36

X is the product of the top two numbers.
Y is the square of x.

266 Black

267 B 27

Starting top left, the letters progress through
the alphabet, omitting 2 letters each time. The
numbers represent the sum of the positions in
the alphabet of the missing letters. When the end
of the alphabet is reached, return to A as if the
letters were written in a circle.

268

269 5 and 5

Here the spacing may have confused you. Had the
digits been placed as follows:

11	13	12	16	13
19	14	22	15	25

you would probably have recognized that there were two alternate sequences, one ascending 1 at a time (11, 12, 13, 14, 15) and the other ascending 3 at a time (13, 16, 19, 22, 25).

270 A = 31 B = 26 C = 36
Examination of the numbers given shows that each number is obtained by multiplying the opposite top number by five and adding one. In the first circle 5 × 3 + 1 = 16 and 5 × 4 + 1 = 21. In the second circle 5 × 6 + 1 = 31 and 5 times 5 + 1 = 26. In the third circle 5 × 1 + 1 = 6 and 5 times 7 + 1 = 36.

271 41 46
Start top left and move along the top row, then back along the second, etc. in the sequence +2, − 1, +3, +2, -1.

272 Taking alternate digits:
9 + 7 + 5 + 4 + 3 = 28
8 + 6 + 2 + 1 = 17

As the difference between the sums of these two digits is 11, the number is divisible by 11 exactly. This would also apply if the difference between the sums of the two digits was any multiple of 11.

273

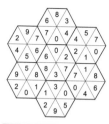

274

275

4	1	6	5	2	9	3	8	7
5	2	8	7	3	4	1	9	6
7	3	9	8	6	1	5	2	4
1	4	7	2	8	5	9	6	3
3	8	2	9	4	6	7	1	5
6	9	5	3	1	7	8	4	2
8	7	4	6	9	3	2	5	1
9	6	3	1	5	2	4	7	8
2	5	1	4	7	8	6	3	9

276

9 3		3 1		3 9		9 5
3 1		5 9		2 7		4 1
1 2 5 7		9 4		1 6 2		
	6 8 2 3 1 4 5					
2 9		9 3 1		1 7		
1 2 8		5 7 9		4 1 2		
4 3 9 2 1			3 7		8 9	
		7 1			1 5	
6 1		9 3		2 9 8		1 3
9 2 5		9 8 6		9 2 8		
	9 4		7 3 4		6 9	
	4 5 7 3 1 2 6					
8 2 6		6 1		5 7 9 8		
3 1		9 8		8 3		1 5
9 7		7 9		2 1		7 9

277 104

Divide the number inside the shape by the number of sides of the shape. Thus 9, divided by 3 (sides of the triangle) gives 3; 20 divided by 4 (sides of the square) gives 5, and so on. You then arrive at the progression: 3, 5, 7, 9, 11, and 13. Therefore in number 6, which is an octagon, the number inside should be 104, which divided by 8, gives 13— the final number of the progression.

278

15	6	10	14
11	4	8	2
13	1	T	12
3	9	5	7

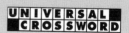